MARS
The Dusty Planet

by Ellen Lawrence

Consultants:

Suzy Gazlay, MA
Recipient, Presidential Award for Excellence in Science Teaching

Kevin Yates
Fellow of the Royal Astronomical Society

Published in 2014 by Ruby Tuesday Books Ltd.

Editor: Mark J. Sachner
Designer: Emma Randall

Photo Credits:
NASA: Cover, 4–5, 6, 8, 10–11, 12–13, 15 (top), 15
(bottom), 16–17, 18–19, 20–21. Ruby Tuesday Books:
7, 22. Shutterstock: 9, 14–15.

Library of Congress Control Number: 2013939816

ISBN 978-1-909673-10-6

Printed and published in the United States of America

For further information including rights and
permissions requests, please contact our Customer
Service Department at 877-337-8577.

Contents

Words shown in **bold** in the text are
explained in the glossary.

Welcome to Mars

You are millions of miles from Earth.

Beneath your feet, the ground is dusty and reddish-brown.

The sky is pinkish-orange.

Icy winds are blowing, and it's colder than the North Pole in December.

You look around and see mountains that are many miles high.

Welcome to the **planet** Mars!

No humans have actually visited Mars, but robots have. This picture of Mars was taken by a robot called *Opportunity*.

Pinkish-orange sky

A mountain

The surface of Mars

The **soil** on Mars looks red because it contains lots of **rust**.

5

The Solar System

Mars is moving through space at nearly 54,000 miles per hour (87,000 km/h).

It is moving in a big circle around the Sun.

Mars is one of eight planets circling the Sun.

The planets are Mercury, Venus, our home planet Earth, Mars, Jupiter, Saturn, Uranus, and Neptune.

Icy **comets** and large rocks, called **asteroids**, are also moving around the Sun.

Together, the Sun, the planets, and other space objects are called the **solar system**.

Most of the asteroids in the solar system are in a ring called the asteroid belt.

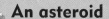
An asteroid

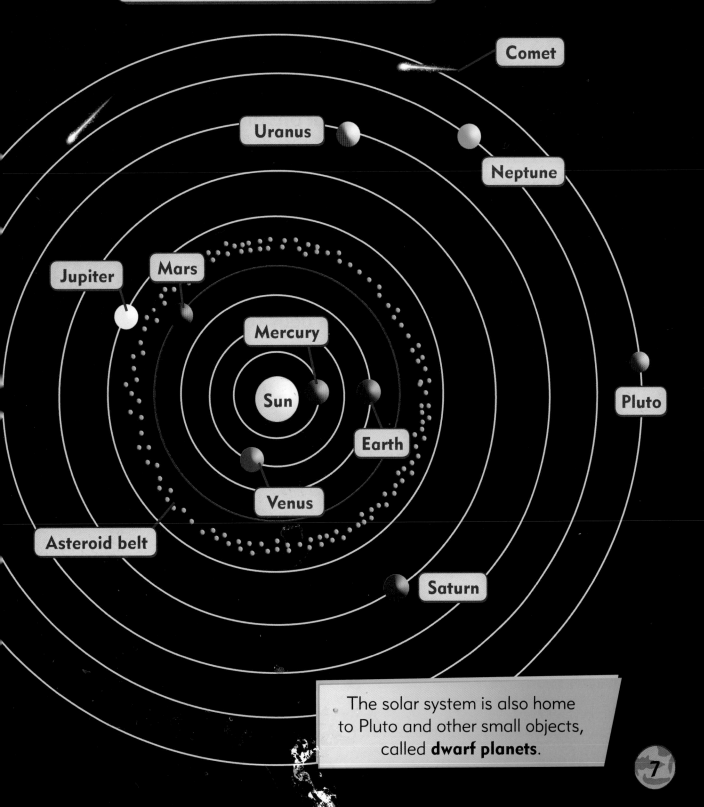

The Solar System
Mars is the fourth planet from the Sun.

Comet

Uranus

Neptune

Jupiter

Mars

Mercury

Sun

Earth

Venus

Pluto

Asteroid belt

Saturn

The solar system is also home to Pluto and other small objects, called **dwarf planets**.

Mars' Amazing Journey

The time it takes a planet to **orbit**, or circle, the Sun once is called its year.

Earth takes just over 365 days to orbit the Sun, so a year on Earth lasts 365 days.

Mars is farther from the Sun than Earth, so it must make a much longer journey.

It takes Mars about 687 Earth days to orbit the Sun.

This means that a year on Mars is nearly twice as long as one on Earth!

As a planet orbits the Sun, it also spins, or **rotates**, like a top.

Mars

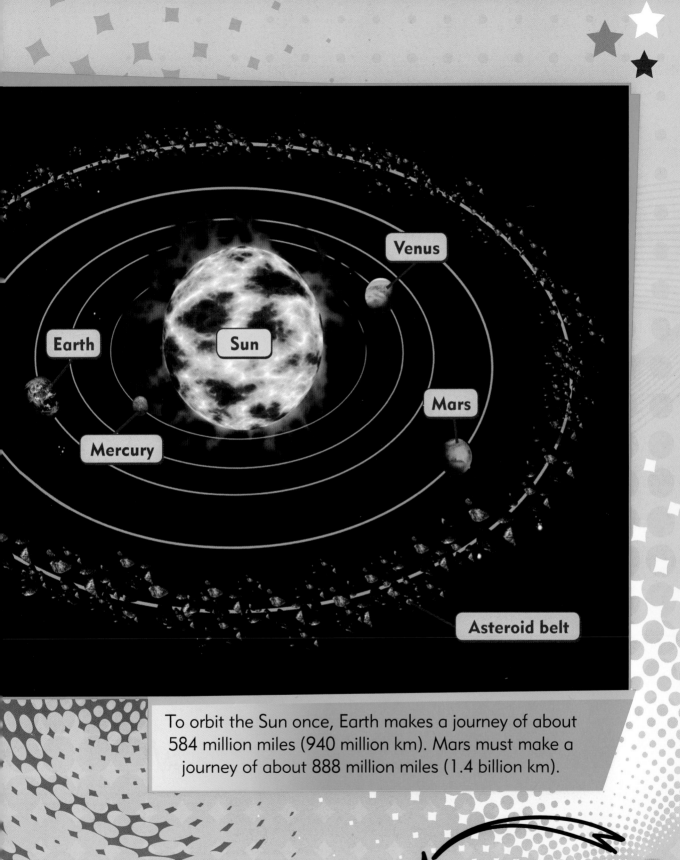

Earth

Sun

Venus

Mercury

Mars

Asteroid belt

To orbit the Sun once, Earth makes a journey of about 584 million miles (940 million km). Mars must make a journey of about 888 million miles (1.4 billion km).

A Closer Look at Mars

Mars is one of Earth's closest neighbors in space, but it is a very different world.

The surface of Mars looks like a dusty, rocky **desert**.

Mars is also a very stormy planet.

The planet's fast winds blow dust up into the sky.

This makes the sky look pinkish-orange.

Sometimes, the whole planet is covered with one giant dust storm!

Earth

Mars

Mars is smaller than Earth. If Earth were the size of a baseball, Mars would be the size of a ping pong ball.

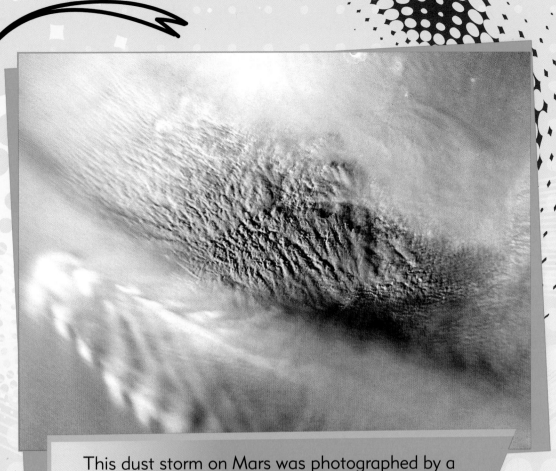

This dust storm on Mars was photographed by a spacecraft flying above the planet.

This picture shows a huge dust devil on Mars. A dust devil is a whirlwind made of dust.

Solar System Record Breakers

Mars is home to the tallest mountain and the deepest **canyon** on any planet in the solar system.

The mountain is a giant **volcano** that is about 14 miles (22 km) high.

It's so large that if it were set down on Earth, it would cover all of Arizona.

Mars' gigantic canyon is 125 miles (200 km) wide.

It is three times as deep as the Grand Canyon!

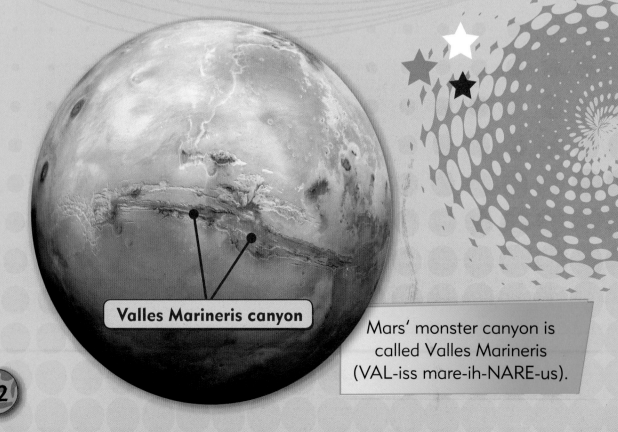

Valles Marineris canyon

Mars' monster canyon is called Valles Marineris (VAL-iss mare-ih-NARE-us).

Mars' massive volcano is called
Olympus Mons (oh-LIM-pus MAHNS).

The Sun

Olympus Mons

Surface of Mars

Today, Olympus Mons does not erupt anymore.
When the volcano was alive, super-hot liquid
rock, called lava, flowed down its sides.

Mars' Tiny Companions

Mars has two tiny companions that stay close to the planet as it orbits the Sun.

These two rocky moons are called Phobos (FOH-bohss) and Deimos (DEE-mohss).

Unlike Earth's Moon, which is round, Mars' moons look like lumpy potatoes.

Phobos and Deimos are orbiting Mars.

Phobos is so close to Mars, it takes just eight hours to orbit the planet.

Deimos is farther away and orbits Mars once every 30 hours.

Deimos is only about 9 miles (14 km) across.

Mars' largest moon, Phobos, is only
about 17 miles (27 km) across.

A Mission to Mars

Scientists have sent several robots to Mars to study the planet.

Some of these robots, called Mars rovers, move around on the surface of Mars.

Curiosity is a car-sized rover that landed on Mars in August 2012.

Scientists on Earth use computers to tell *Curiosity* where to go and what to do.

Curiosity is millions of miles from Earth.

This means it can take up to 21 minutes for the scientists' commands to reach the rover.

This picture shows scientists at **NASA** building *Curiosity*.

Rocket

Curiosity was placed into a spacecraft. The spacecraft blasted off from Earth aboard a rocket on November 26, 2011.

The spacecraft carried *Curiosity* from Earth to Mars. The journey took just over eight months.

The Robotic Rover

Curiosity's mission is to study soil and rocks on Mars.

The robotic rover found clues in rock that show there was once water on the planet.

Living things need water to survive.

This means that tiny living things, called **microbes**, might once have been able to live on Mars.

Curiosity is also studying Mars to help scientists plan future missions.

These missions could include sending humans to visit the planet!

Curiosity has cameras, tools, and science equipment on board. The robot drills into rocks. Then it collects and tests the powdered rock it has made.

Powdered rock

Curiosity takes photos of itself on Mars. The robot beams the photos back to Earth so scientists can be sure it is in good shape!

Curiosity

Mars Fact File

Here are some key facts about Mars, the fourth planet from the Sun.

Discovery of Mars

Mars can be seen in the sky without a telescope. People have known it was there since ancient times.

How Mars got its name

Mars is named after the Roman god of war.

Planet sizes

This picture shows the sizes of the solar system's planets compared to each other.

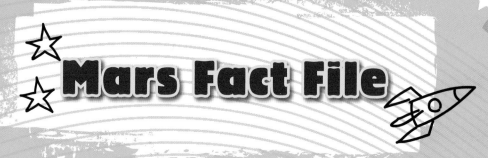

Sun · Mercury · Earth · Venus · Mars · Jupiter · Saturn · Uranus · Neptune

Mars' size

4,212 miles (6,779 km) across

How long it takes for Mars to rotate once

Nearly 25 hours

Mars' distance from the Sun

The closest Mars gets to the Sun is 128,409,598 miles (206,655,215 km).

The farthest Mars gets from the Sun is 154,865,853 miles (249,232,432 km).

Length of Mars' orbit around the Sun

877,992,283 miles (1,429,085,052 km)

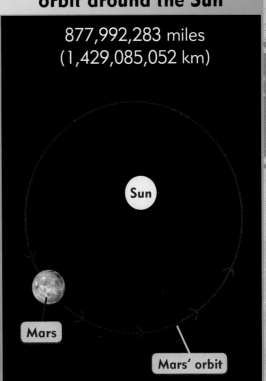

Sun

Mars

Mars' orbit

Average speed at which Mars orbits the Sun

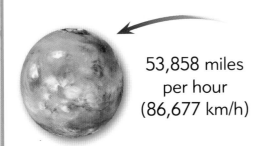

53,858 miles per hour (86,677 km/h)

Length of a year on Mars

687 Earth days

Mars' moons

Mars has two moons:

Deimos

Phobos

 ## Temperature on Mars

Highest: 23°F (−5°C)

Lowest: −125°F (−87°C)

Get Crafty
Build a Robot Explorer

You can make your own robot explorer!

Here are some ideas for things you might use to make a robot:

- Empty boxes, cartons, or bottles
- Toilet paper tubes
- Clean, used aluminum foil
- Any other materials you can think of

Here's one example of a robot rover, but you can create your own design. Think about:

- What shape will your robot be?
- How will it move around?
- What tools and equipment does it have?
- What tasks might it perform?

Here are some items you might need when making your robot:

- Scissors
- White glue
- Tape
- Paints and a paintbrush
- An adult to help with cutting

Glossary

asteroid (AS-teh-royd) A large rock that is orbiting the Sun. An asteroid can be as small as a car or bigger than a mountain.

canyon (KAN-yun) A deep valley with steep sides.

comet (KAH-mit) A space object made of ice, rock, and dust that is orbiting the Sun.

desert (DEH-zurt) A rocky or sandy place where there is no water, or very little water. A desert can be very hot or very cold.

dwarf planet (DWARF PLAN-et) A round object in space that is orbiting the Sun. Dwarf planets are much smaller than the eight main planets.

microbe (MY-krobe) A living thing that is so tiny it can't be seen with your eyes. The germs that make people sick are types of microbes.

NASA (NA-suh) A group of scientists and space experts in the United States. NASA studies space and builds spacecraft. The letters in NASA stand for "National Aeronautics and Space Administration."

orbit (OR-bit) To circle, or move around, another object.

planet (PLAN-et) A large object in space that is orbiting the Sun. Some planets, such as Mars and Earth, are made of rock. Others, such as Jupiter, are made of gases and liquids.

rotate (ROH-tate) To spin around.

rust (RUHST) A reddish-orange, crumbly substance that forms on metal.

soil (SOYL) The crumbly material that covers the ground in many places. Soil is made mostly of tiny bits of rock.

solar system (SOH-ler SIS-tem) The Sun and all the objects that orbit it, such as planets, their moons, asteroids, and comets.

volcano (vol-KAY-noh) A mountain or hill that has an opening on it from which hot, liquid rock can erupt onto the surface of a planet or another body in space.

Index

Read More

Hughes, Catherine D.
*First Big Book of Space
(National Geographic Little
Kids)*. Washington, D.C.:
The National Geographic
Society (2012).

James, Lincoln.
*Mars: The Red Planet
(Our Solar System)*.
New York: Gareth Stevens
(2011).

Learn More Online

To learn more about Mars, go to
www.rubytuesdaybooks.com/mars